BRIT OF AN AMERICAN

You Know You're British Living in America When...

Written by Yvette Durham

Illustrated by Fearn Elder

Copyright

A Brit of an American: You Know You're British Living in America When...: by Yvette Durham

Published by Yvette Durham

Longwood, FL 32779

Cover by Rejenne Pavon/www.rejenne.com

Illustration by Fearn Elder

Author's Bio Photo by David Maybury

ISBN: 9798426152106

Printed in United States of America

First Edition

Dedicated with love and gratitude to my American husband, Eric, and our Brit of American children, Alex and Sophie.

Y'all have taught me the true value of orthodontists, bulk-buying and hurricane parties. I really am the better Brit for it.

CONTENTS

INTRODUCTION

There are several things I've noticed about Brits living in America. Firstly, we're secretly united by our terminally British reactions to all things thoroughly American, such as does 'rowt' mean the same thing as 'route?' Is there anything that intimidating yet indispensable garbage disposal won't shred to bits? And do Americans even like the taste of coffee, or are they just in it for the flavored creamer?

Secondly, we stateside Brits instinctively tend to huddle together, often within the virtual arms of a social media expat group or four. There we indulge in a bit of sneaky food porn, frequently posted by members visiting the UK. We collectively drool over pictures of fry-ups *with* baked beans, steamy Sunday roasts and slow-motion videos featuring custard being teasingly poured over treacle tarts.

Thirdly, as much as many of us proclaim our undying love and allegiance to America and bah-humbug any thoughts of returning to Blighty, we remain partial to a therapeutic, tea-sponsored grumble over our adopted homeland in the way that only we Brits do: *gleefully*.

Then there's Brits who may be fresh-off-the-boaters (but can even be those of us who have seen decades of proper US summers), who seem to be suffering from a very acute and sometimes debilitating case of homesickness for Britain. We may even question whatever state of mind led us to say 'sod it, let's move to America, why ever not?'

Once we've sobered up and landed stateside we realize with a shudder of horror that our comfort zones ditched us somewhere over the Atlantic. Here we are, in all our sensitive emotionally-repressed glory, in a New World which appears noisy, confrontational and with no NHS for us in those moments we make very whoopsie-daisy choices at 3am.

Looking back, America makes Britain seem cozy, obliging and delightfully free from I-can-kill-you-wildlife and monstrous bloodcurdling weather conditions. It doesn't take us long to work out that the USA is designed for competitors, bravehearts, doers, people who like to shine in all the best lights. Oh dear; these are not adjectives we'd use to describe Brits. We're severely under-qualified Americans.

But linger here long enough, smushed in all things American, and we start to observe our thoughts and behaviors altering from the inside out. We find ourselves not fully British, and definitely not fully American, but a *Brit of an American.*

No matter how long you've been in the States, or where you are in the expat satisfaction spectrum, this book is for you. We'll visit various aspects of living in America that have the potential to send us a *brit* bonkers including eating out, home life, the booze culture, driving, Christmas and much more. From a glance at typical life scenarios and our classic British reactions, you'll know that far from a freak of nature you are indeed one of us, and we're all in this culturally befuddled state together.

As you'll see the bulk of the chapters are in bite-sized portions. (Remember those?) Basically, you could stick '*You Know You're British Living in America When...*' in front of the statements and they'd make a certain kind of sense. As such this book makes an excellent addition to the magazine rack beside the toilet. Or perhaps for back seat drivers on a lengthy road trip, you know, so you can give the driver a bit of a rest.

There are also a few quirky chapters thrown in including an expectation versus reality chapter and an A-Z of homesickness hacks, for those days you just need morale-boosting kick up the bum. We'll also explore the ways Americans and Brits differ and how this can ultimately prove to be very advantageous for us. Then there's a quiz to determine how Americanized you sound.

Before we get stuck in, I must welcome any Americans, and caveat everything you may read with a blanket 'sorry, hope we can still be friends, I love you really.' I'd also like to salute you if you're an American who's decided to befriend, date or marry one of us Brits. (Love can be a cruel, indiscriminate business, I know.) I hope this book serves as a bit of a heads-up on what you might be letting yourself in for. You may have noticed that underneath our perfectly cheery and polite veneers we actually have a *lot* of thoughts and feelings thumping about. These pages are a low-risk exploration of everything we so convincingly repress so you'll be ready for your Brit's reactions to your country, which may not always be pretty, but we do know by now you're extremely proud of.

If you're an Anglophile or an Americanophile (yes, apparently the latter really is a thing), or just a bit curious, really, then come o' in too. This is the juicy secrets of living in the States that extend beyond topical tourist visits. And although specifically tailored with Brits in mind, this book will undoubtedly resonate with other nationalities living in the USA.

* Disclaimer: no Americans were harmed in the making of this book (aside from my very patient husband who made an excellent sounding board). Admittedly, a few Brits were interviewed with subpar tea-time supplies, but there's not much we can do about that over here. Enjoy...

A Brit About Me...

With my maiden name of Yvette Eleanor Scott, my initials already had me marked out as a candidate for saying YES to America, Ye Land of Opportunity. Serendipitously, then, I met my American husband in Sierra Leone, Africa. He was an officer in the US Army, I was a rather adventurous/foolish air hostess based at that moment in time in Crawley. Probably due to the heady combination of a fiery African sun, generously-laced cocktails and the apparent aphrodisiac of a British accent, he took a life-binding chance on me.

We married in a very chilly church wedged atop a hill in the heart of Dorset, surrounded by our family and friends. We'd hired an old red London bus to transport the guests to the wedding. The Americans couldn't contain their squeals over the 'hobbit-like' thatched cottages that clung to the winding lanes en route. No wonder...

After arriving in a very flat, very barren Kansas as a young bride, I thought 'Golly. I'm really not sure this was such a good idea, after all,' but probably with a lot more swear words.

Everyone and everything that gave my life meaning was gone. No more mum to run home to when I'd spent my last tenner down the pub. In America, I couldn't even ask where the loo was without invoking a fifteen-minute conversation about which peculiar part of the planet I'd sprung from. And, anyway, what's a loo?

I honored my instinct to simply hide for a few months and live vicariously through streaming British soaps. Eventually, I peeped out of my burrow, took yoga classes for sanity's sake and, even more so to that end, joined a meet-up expat group called 'I'm British: What the F*ck am I doing in Kansas?!'

After moving to Colorado, I braced to dive headfirst into this other version of American life. My husband deployed to Afghanistan for the longest years of our lives, meaning home didn't feel like home anymore. And, with a nine-month-old baby son, hibernation was no longer a sensible option. Although I knew diddly about motherhood, I had grasped that babies needed fresh air as well as feeding and watering. I bribed myself with the promise of any decadent thing I wanted from the bakery and an afternoon's mindless telly session if I could heave together the courage to join a group or two. Before I let myself over-think it, I was a member of *Mothers of Preschoolers* and *Toastmasters* (for me, a sort of *Rosetta Stone* for Brits trying to speak the American lingo). I attached myself to the social happenings with the other Army wives and together we even climbed Pikes Peak mountain, 14,000 feet above sea level. (I'd hope that vantage point would allow me to see the White Cliffs of Dover. It didn't.)

New relationships slowly started to melt much of the outward signs of homesickness, at least. Diving in (or belly-flopping, more like,) was a formula I subscribed to when we moved to Florida after hubby's retirement from the Army. I joined a yoga studio before I'd even unpacked the moving boxes. Now-largely due to the fact that Americans are very partial to listening to a British accent for an uninterrupted hour- I'm a yoga instructor and teacher mentor.

The once upon a time culture that made me go *what the bloody hell, America,* is becoming familiar, even-dare I say- *normal.*

Yep; fifteen years, several moves and two children later, I'm pleased to report that I'm living my best life. I'm still slightly in awe of my British/American double vision, which lets me recognize and relish the best of both worlds. It's also fun to pick my allegiance to which country, given the situation. For example, I'm usually channeling my American side when it comes to sporting events. Except for Wimbledon, then I whip out the *Pimms* and my still-British accent attempts and utterly fails to sound like Kate Middleton, only posher.

I'll take the forehead wrinkles, well-grooved from a permanently wide-eyed expression that leaving my safe little birth island has left me with. (Botox's available on every corner anyway.) The initial stress of immigration has been well worth it.

I offer this book at the intersection of feeling equal parts British and American. As such I'm ideally poised to remember the dizzying effect of dunking someone so British into an all-

American environment. Yet also far enough along in my own American Adventure to feel irretrievably and unapologetically Americanized.

Although my daughter still notices that everything I watch is set in England and/or with the Queen in it, I say *cheers* to we Brit of Americans, and here's to us thriving stateside.

Food and Drink

'The only foreign language you'll really need to learn in America is ingredient labels. But for beginners, here's my advice: if you ever see more than seven unpronounceable words on the label, leave it to its shelf life.' Will you go bananas? Quite possibly. But at least you won't have to worry about reading labels in the fruit and veg section.'

- Joanna, Georgia/Somerset, nobly sticking to her good-food-only mantra, but unfortunately spending 64% of her paycheck in the health food store.

- It can't be your fault that your herbs die after only a month; it must be the American soil.

- Netflix documentaries about America's meat industry scare you into becoming a vegan (except for bacon and Sunday lunches, of course).

- You and your British-bought skinny jeans are no longer a good fit.

- Emerging from the British shop three hours later and $657 poorer.

- Nah, you don't lift weights, you just pop to the supermarket and heave condiments into the trolley.

- Threatening to leave the country immediately after discovering the sliced bread you just bought contains high fructose corn syrup.

- You're well and truly sorry for ever taking spreadable butter for granted.

- Not even your piss-poor inner teenager would have imagined that the no-frills German supermarket would one day become your food-Mecca.

- Fighting back the tears; somebody's beaten you to the last jar of *Branston Pickle.*

- *What you want*: baked beans.

  What you find: baked beans with brown sugar; maple and bacon baked beans; thick, sickly, molasses-soaked baked beans swimming in honey; vegetarian baked beans; baked beans with suspicious sausagy particles perhaps once pertaining to a pig.

  Result: lonely toast.

- Checking the supermarket's busy times to avoid too many absentminded trolley drivers.

- *Eggplants*: And here's us Brits believing eggs plopped out of a chicken's bottom...

- The appeal of boiling peanuts is still utterly lost on you.

- In a bid to help your body bugger on despite the American food industry's best efforts, Elevenses becomes the number of vitamins you take on a daily basis.

- The supermarket's international aisle is your absolute favorite.

- Hurrah! Thank you global pandemic and national lockdown for finally bringing us online grocery shopping.

- Thanks to pesticide-sprayed produce you fear tremors, migraines, kidney damage, neurotoxicity and asthma may become your new five a day.

- Profusely apologizing to Mother Earth for forgetting your Bag for Life and therefore being handed sixteen doubled-up plastic bags to carry home three small items.

- Feeling confused by your handwritten shopping list- the chips are down- but do you need more chips or crisps?

- Boiled sweets (thanks to boiling peanuts) sounds more off-putting than tempting to your Brit of an American brain.

- Fluoride in the tap water? What a gnashing idea.

- Wondering how the French feel after tasting the soups, mustards and chips the Americans so sweetly named after them.

- Taking six years to realize cilantro and coriander are the same thing.

- Deciding saying prayers before a meal must be an American's last-minute line of defense against all the butter and cheese about to be received.

- Regrettably, half a pint becomes the measuring jug in your kitchen.

- Note to self: best not ask the supermarket assistant ever again for squirty cream.

- Assimilation means eating biscuits and gravy and actually really rather enjoying the odd combination of scones and bread sauce.

- Thinking-look- if you really want to name something after the French, why not call that big long sandwich there a baguette?

- Counting 153 ingredients on the ready-meal you just bought and deciding to feed it to your family would be tantamount to manslaughter.

- Ordering a medium-sized popcorn and subsequently missing the whole movie.

- Pizza: oh please, no, not again.

- Thoroughly disappointing your well-mannered British side by eating dinner out of a plastic microwaveable dish.

- Wondering which will come sooner; socialist healthcare or you drinking iced tea on a regular basis?

- You're beginning to realize why bathrooms contain magazines as on-toilet entertainment, thanks to the time it takes to offload the standard American caloric intake.

- You've been here so long that you can't for the life of you remember what the British equivalent to cornstarch is.

- Morning coffee is your new afternoon tea.

- Boston Harbor 1773: they call it a tea party; you call it an outrage.

- Your version of spilling the beans is admitting you still drink instant coffee at home.

- Absolutely loving drive-thru coffee chains; such an inspired way of stimulating British sarcasm on-the-go.

- You strongly believe that if you took away all the '*I'll-take-a-Grande-iced-coffee-ten-pumps-vanilla-six-pumps-hazelnut-eight-pumps-skinny-mocha-a-splash-of-almondmilk-ice-double-blended*' sorts of people, America's social problems would quietly slink away overnight.

Hanging out

'Only hours after leaving Heathrow, here I was, surrounded by agonizingly laid-back Americans with resonant voices and definite ideas, who only seem to have one mode of being; loud and proud. Of course, the most disarming thing of all is they're so strikingly honest.'
–Tom, Illinois/Wiltshire, clearly ready for a bit of a lie-down.

- Immediately warming to any American who says they've been to Britain.

- You firmly wish 'don't talk to strangers' applied to adults too.

- Deciding it's time to upgrade your 'I'm fine, thanks' to 'I'm great!' to make sure you don't come across as grumpy as you feel.

- After a few social occasions, hungrily reading books such as *How to Win Friends & Influence People*, yet still feeling desperately British.

- Only noticing since moving to the US that you have a rather nasally nervous giggle.

- Spending the next nine years regretting befriending an expat solely on the qualifying factor that they were British.

- American: 'Where are you from? Australia?'
  You: 'Close. But no, Britain.'
  American: 'Britain's in En-ger-land, right?'

- Secretly enjoying being told to self-isolate during Coronavirus.

- You don't think there's anything at all blocking the average American's throat chakra.

- Your dentist's children refer to you as their Tooth Fairy; or was it Fairy Godmother?

- Never feeling like more of a far-out hippie than during election time.

- Eau D' Brit: Just like sharks can smell the faint hint of odor from faraway prey, you too can sniff out a fellow Brit from over a mile away.

- The only time you can't remember your social security number is when you need to.

- You become a 'good listener.'

- A chinwag is now a solo but literal way to express your disapproval.

- Never quite knowing what to do with yourself during the American National Anthem.

- Your superpower is your accent.

- Being asked by American acquaintances if you happen to know their friend John Smith from London.

- It's amazing how patriotic for Britain you've become now you actually don't live there.

- Suddenly feeling a bit silly for ending conversations with multiple byes.

- Profusely apologizing to a parking meter for giving you a concussion, a black- eye and a broken fibula.

- You decide the British translation for authenticity is a *brit* too much information.

- Never managing to get passed a cashier without discussing your British origins.

- You've told so many geographically-challenged Americans you're from London that you start sounding like a character from a Charles Dickens novel.

- Your religion and your expat group are practically the same thing.

- Working on your conflict management skills by delegating an American to make the complaint.

- Brexit: pretending you know what you're talking about, but secretly you're just as baffled.

- Parties in Britain= Dressy events with lots of alcohol to blot out social awkwardness.
  Parties in US= Casual bring-your-own-dish affairs, ample plasticware; no alcohol necessary.

- Taking up a spot of hyperbole; it's amazing how awesome and great everything is over here.

- To you, freedom of expression means the right to remain silent.

- Thanks to your iPhone's predictable text, your guests come over to your house with the expectation of cupcakes, not a cuppa.

- Reserving your passionately strong political thoughts for social media.

- Batting blush-inducing compliments away from well-meaning Americans as if you're swatting flies.

- To your mind in a state of cultural transition, a 'good sesh' refers less to happy hour down the pub, and more to the time passed on your therapist's sofa.

DRIVING DOUBTS

Dad: 'Can't you just catch the train, rather than sit in all that traffic?'
James: 'I'd honestly rather catch the flu than do public transport over here, dad.'
-James, North Carolina/Norfolk, really trying not to drive himself mad.

- Despite yourself, you've grown rather fond of Radio Country FM.

- 'Would you like a ride?' still seems a rather indecent proposal to your Brit of an American brain.

- Buying a shiny big-grilled SUV for the price of a hatchback in the UK and trying really hard not to brag about it on *Facebook.*

- You've long since forgotten how to negotiate roundabouts.

- Your favorite way to stress yourself out is to try and turn right on a red light.

- Now you're laughing too when Brits refer to your car as a 'people carrier.'

- Taking your US drivers test and being pretty sure you could have passed it in your sleep.

- In your experience, traffic lights can turn five miles into half a morning's drive.

- Being asked for directions and pretending you're a Brit on holiday that hasn't got a clue.

- Reasons for putting a British license plate on the front of your car:-
  a. It's acceptably patriotic
  b. Drivers may give you a wider berth
  c. There are a lot of anglophiles out there, so if you're single, this could be more effective than online dating

- The moment you discover the banging songs on the radio belongs to an evangelical Christian station.

- Wanting to grab the steering wheel when your otherwise very sensible friend starts texting while driving.

- Seeing a helmet-less motorcyclist in the other lane and slowing down to tortoise-speed for the sake of his mum.

- It'll forever be a novelty nose-diving into any parking space in your over-sized car, and yet always landing inside the white lines.

- Worrying about developing deep vein thrombosis every time you use the drive-thru cash point.

- You would take the bus but you're not sure if you're broke enough to qualify.

- Spending thirty minutes at the four-way stop sign politely letting every other car go.

- Spying a police patrol vehicle in the highway median and praying the officer isn't the gun-ho law and order type.

- You practice dismounting from the new family truck as if it were a horse in a Jane Austen film.

- Watching yet another car ignore a pedestrian waiting to cross and assuming the Americans must only stop for actual zebras.

- Roadside billboards teach your children everything they need to know about sex.

- Nowadays you rent cars, not hire them.

- You're chuffed to announce that your car has even more cup holders than passenger seats.

- After fourteen days, two hours and fifty-six minutes, you finally see the leaving-the-state sign.

- Spending thirty minutes searching for the gearstick which some tool drilled into the side of the steering wheel.

- It takes an awfully long time to switch out an old car tyre for a new car tire, but spell-check eventually grinds you down.

- 143% of your high blood pressure is down to Americans forgetting their cars come with indicators.

- Thanks to your dogged determination to drive a manual car, you now have an inbuilt anti-millennial theft device.

- You're certainly pleased MOT tests are nothing more than a speck of dust in your rearview mirror now.

- Your first bumper sticker: Queen Elizabeth II Take the Wheel 2024.

Great British Expectations of America Versus Reality

No doubt our American chums come to Britain with the utopian lifestyle delusions of *Downton Abbey* and *Harry Potter*. Never mind that one is based on the upper echelons of society a hundred years ago, and the other is completely fantastical and all about wizards.

Naughty, lying televisions. Tell 'e the truth would you, instead of these visions.

And equally, when we land in America, gingerly emerging into the New World, our own media and telly-fed exposure can present a pretty seismic gulf between what we expect and what we actually get...

Style-a-ballistic

Expectation…

Reality...

Wearing fashionable clothes is not a national law over here. Because of this oversight, people are left to their own dressing-devices. This means anything goes (even though it doesn't).

Home Strife

Expectation...

Reality...

The 'lived-in look' seems to be very popular, and thankfully it's effortless to achieve.

Making Progress?

Expectation...

Reality...

Well, variety has indeed made things spicy.

Land(e)scape

Expectation...

Reality...

Hello Mr. Bison, or are you a buffalo? Would you be so kind as to direct me to the nearest watering hole please, 'The Bull's Head' p'raps?

To be Wealthy, or Not to be Wealthy?

Expectation...

Reality…

Wowzies. America seems to have the whole world in its hands, from First to Third.

Home Sweet Home?

'My house is a dream! The closet's twice as big as my old studio flat. But the downside is the homes over here don't seem to be made very substantially. In fact, I'm pretty sure the Big Bad Wolf would have no trouble blowing it down. And in the US, that huffy-puffy wolf is called a tornado, and I happen to live right up its alley.'- Karen, Kansas/Leicester, digging deep in the relative safety of her basement.

- Giving that obstinate *Alexa* a jolly loud tut because she still refuses to understand your accent.

- Adopting a love/hate relationship with your garbage disposal and spending many interesting moments getting to know what it enjoys eating (such as your best spoons).

- In your opinion, the distance between your front door and mailbox at the end of the driveway constitutes ample exercise for a small to mid-sized dog.

- Moving to a southern state and finding it alright; apparently, usually-considered- conservative-you is now the only radical liberal in town.

- Never knowing what 'keeping up with the Joneses' really means until your neighbor buys a prettier car than yours.

- Experiencing the frenzied desire to purchase lesser-known kitchen gadgets because where would you be without a cob corn stripper or salad spinner in your life?

- Finding the air conditioning 'drafty' and therefore only allowing it to be turned on if the internal temperature causes your face to melt.

- To you, there's a direct link between an American's tendency to over-dramatize situations and a lack of homes owning electric kettles.

- You quickly learn that Homeowners Associations are like Big Brother, only more controlling.

- Establishing early on that if you're ever going to fit in, you really do need to create a fifty square foot shrine to America's demigod- *coffee.*

- Still having no idea which room a den refers to.

- To you, the TV channel PBS is an acronym for Pleasant British Series.

- Scoffing at how housework used to take forty minutes back home in your bijou British flat; now it's more like four days.

- That Tupperware dilemma: keep it, or return to neighbor?

- Trying to convert every tradesperson who enters your home to the sweet wonders of builders tea.

- You have an ornament collecting dust in your bathroom called a water pix.

- Strongly suspecting American TV commercials have given you a nasty case of ADD.

- Having an overwhelming urge to turn your home into a cozy British nest with bunting, union jack pillows and scenic pictures of red buses.

- You wonder how you ever got by back in Britain with only a drawer for a freezer.

- Even though you're the least frigid person you'll ever meet, you still can't see how three large fridges per household are not enough to feed a family of four.

- By now, your brain has memorized the Celsius to Fahrenheit conversion chart.

- You often get told off for opening the windows.

- There's a rustic farmhouse sign in your dining room saying 'no shirt, no shoes, no service.'

- Refusing to clean your bath with household products because you really do rather value your lungs and eyesight.

- They may call it a laundry room, but it'll always be a utility room to you.

- Finding it difficult to disguise your amusement when an American refers to your 1970s home as 'old.'

- Realizing that, when invited, Americans will indeed make themselves at home.

- Since living here, you've come such a long way in being able to express your feelings that you can now comfortably yell at the radio.

- Your kitty's new way of getting catatonic involves sniffing lawns labeled 'caution-pesticide applied.'

- If you ever return to Britain, you're taking your measuring cups and spoons with you.

- You're convinced you could pop a three-piece suite on the curb and those lovely bin men would still take it away.

- Now you're happily settled in your new American home, you decide it's about time to stick a great big British flag on the front porch.

Boozing

'There's a seedy, unwelcoming malice to bars here. There's no highly social relationship with getting merry amongst friends in cozy pubs. Those who do tend to drink heavily and regularly in America are often relegated to drab underground rooms, filled with the foggy air of cigarette smoke, poverty and despair. But at least the drinks are strong and cheap.'

–Sophie, Georgia/Hampshire, still searching for a local.

- Being completely incapable of enjoying any alcoholic beverage served in a big red plastic cup.

- Your new idea of throwing a wobbly is necking a jelly vodka shot.

- After surveying America's drinking culture, you decide 95% of your British family and friends back home are alcohol-dependent at best.

- Reading the bar's cocktail menu with as much passion as the Kama Sutra.

- You really want to ask the barperson for sex on the beach, but you're worried they might take it the wrong way.

- Asking for a lager top and receiving a very blank expression.

- You: 'This isn't beer! It's water with an infusion of beer tasting substance; it's probably beer flavored high fructose corn syrup.'

- Saying, 'Just a tiny bit of ice please.' (Don't want to water down the alcohol, do we?)

- As far as you're concerned, hypnotists have got nothing on the power of Sports Bar televisions.

- Martinis in posh glasses; olive you.

- After watching your first Superbowl, you completely understand now why Americans pregame.

- You often order appetizers you don't want so you can use chain restaurants for their fully-stocked bars.

- Reminding yourself to drop certain bar-related terminology; no more getting pissed for you or asking for...cigarettes.

- Your therapist doubles up as the local liquor store owner.

- Go-to drunken slurs usually revolve around the year 1776.

- You've developed a seemingly agreeable tipping method:-
  1. Drink lots and lots
  2. Stab still-legible numbers from the bill into your phone's calculator
  3. Slap a 0 on the end

- It may cost as much as the meal itself, but you're going to order a glass of wine anyway.

- Playing American trivia drinking games equates to your sorry state of inebriation.

- Feeling uniquely qualified for the barperson position at your local pub; you may as well get paid for being there.

- Thanks to social media's memory, your British drinking antics still come back to haunt you.

- *Moonshine*: better not. Not after last time.

- You're such a responsible drinker now that you even watch documentaries about the dangers of alcohol (avec your large glass of *Chardonnay*).

- Feeling like you're winning as a responsible parent because your twelve-year-old child doesn't yet go to the park to drink out of big plastic bottles of cider.

- Silently willing a fellow work colleague to order a glass of wine at the company lunch too.

- *Total Wines* feels like *Toys R'Us* once did.

- The best bit about liquor stores is having your bottle wrapped in a quintessentially American brown paper bag and therefore getting to feel like a drunken outlaw the whole way home.

- Warm British draft ale becomes the stuff of fantasies.

- Being unable to sleep for three days following a drinking session and blaming it on the soda.

- Trying to honestly assess if you'd have moved to America during Prohibition.

- It really isn't flattering anymore to be asked for ID.

- Quitting alcohol and realizing life is magical without it, yet returning home and feeling powerless to resist the seductively-lit alcohol aisle in *Tesco.*

- The naughtiest thing you dare do over here is sneak alcoholic drinks onto the beach.

- Your liver transplant involved moving from Britain to America.

It's Christmas Time! (But Not as We Know it)

'I've managed to source some Christmas crackers for lunch, but there aren't any mince pies in the supermarkets, or supersized tubs of Cheddars or Twiglets to graze on during all that brilliant Christmas telly. There's no goose fat for the roasties; imagine that? Or Boxing Day sales shopping. In fact, there's no such thing as Boxing Day; it's business as usual, as if Christmas was just a momentary daydream. And the topper on the Christmas tree is it's eighty bloody degrees outside.'

–Beth, Central Florida/Birmingham, acclimatizing to her second Christmas stateside.

- Non-negotiable Brit of an American festive viewing: *Love Actually*.

- Managing to source mulled wine and therefore officially announcing you're feeling *Christmassy* (much to everyone's relief).

- You begin putting the decorations up in early November.

- Contemplating adding a pair of reindeer antlers to your car shortly before shaking yourself back to British mode.

- You object to blow-up outdoor decorations on any grounds.

- Your nerves are severely jingled when some cheeky bugger describes your new Christmas jumper as *ugly*.

- These days, you decorate the Christmas tree with less tinsel and more ribbon.

- You think elves on shelves are just creepy; probably another spying tactic from the Homeowners Association.

- The most sensible place to get batteries at Christmas becomes a bulk-buying industrial warehouse.

- You're American enough now to realize pulling off a successful Christmas means you'll have to start planning in June.

- All your American friends are baking like frenzied elves, and you can never figure out why they don't just buy a packet of biscuits.

- Your Christmas wish list:-
  Britbox subscription
  Cath Kidston anything
  Retro British sweets

- Wondering why Americans can't just sap all religious connotations out of the school nativity like we Brits do.

- Going to church and wondering if it really was a Wise Man who decided to use a real baby over a plastic, drop-proof Jesus?

- Did someone fandangle with the melody of *Away in a Manger*? Or did they put something funny in the confirmation wine?

- Now you can personalize Christmas cards with a festive family picture, your ego takes the trouble to send them again.

- Regretting ordering your Christmas cards on photo paper now you've realized what cardstock is.

- Getting overly excited at the Brit store and hastily paying $20 for a tub of *Heroes*.

- Oh dear, it's supermarket squirty cream-gate all over again as you accidentally make rude phallic gestures trying to explain to the produce assistant what a parsnip is.

- Privately debating if your foreign status means you can get away with wishing people a 'Merry Christmas' instead of the more clinical 'Happy Holidays.'

- The thing that puts you off the most is the word: *eggnog*.

- Trying to tell an American that mimosa sounds like a magic spell, not a cocktail of sparkling wine and orange juice.

- American spouse: 'Let's drive through the neighborhood and look at all the Christmas lights!'
  You: 'Right-o. Should we wear sunscreen?'

- Telling your child that Santa has a dairy intolerance-and clearly he's had one too many cookies-what he needs after his tumble down the chimney is a hot toddy and a mince pie.

- Saying: 'I've found a hollandaise packet for the Eggs Benedict, but it contains corn maltodextrin, soy lecithin and monosodium glutamate; are you prepared to risk it?'

- Grammy appears at the front door wearing your favorite 'Move over Santa, here comes Grandma' t-shirt.

- Now stateside, the Queen's Speech gets promoted to unmissable Christmas viewing.

- You bitterly defend the *Fairytale of New York's* lyrical content for small ears.

- Insisting everyone (Americans) wears their cracker hat for the entirety of the Christmas meal, including bathroom excursions.

- Quietly weeping over the absence of your British loved ones; oh how you miss bread sauce and those wee little piggies wrapped in blankets.

- To you, it's perfectly obvious why bite-sized party food never caught on over here.

- You preferred Scrooge before he was visited by the three ghosts.

- Carefully explaining to all American guests again exactly why Christmases are much better in Britain.

- Having a well-earned nap after giving Oscar-worthy performances unwrapping presents you really didn't want.

- Subjecting American guests to a repetitive soundtrack of *Slade* and *Wham* while saying 'never gets old, does it?'

- You always manage to let the Secret Santa side down.

- Being utterly baffled by the American tradition of *going to the cinema on Christmas Day* for several reasons:-
    a. Who, apart from the kids, is sober enough to drive in the first place?
    b. There will be lots of people there
    c. How come you never knew this was a thing until moving here? Going to the cinema on Christmas Day is like being in a surreal universe you have no wish to be a part of

- Waking up on Christmas morning and video calling back home to find British relatives comatosed with drink and turkey tryptophan.

- Utterly failing to rally anyone, save the dog, for the obligatory Christmas Walk.

- Discreetly researching the history of Boxing Day because you also assumed it was about exasperated relatives hitting each other.

A Brit of an American's A-Z of Homesickness Hacks

Missing Britain? Same. Yet for immediate relief from the pangs of nostalgia, let's remind ourselves of all the super-duper benefits a stateside life has to offer...

All-American Breakfast

Bottomless coffee, crunchy hash browns, syrup-drenched pancakes, fresh-baked 'biscuits' and peppery white gravy; this is bound to get you all sunny-side up.

Adventure Awaits

There's forty times more land to romp about in, *yeehaw!*

Al Fresco

Taking us back to atmospheric memories of continental holidays, summery-summers allow us to al fresco at home as if we're ouzo-ing about in Greece.

British Expat TV

Because where would we be without the BBC?

Beaches

The exceedingly clever inclusion of sand and a big round hot yellow ball in the sky to warm everything up is genius (not so good for your egg and cress sarnies though).

Beauty Products

Ulta, Sephora and MAC have been known to reduce British homesickness by about 6000% (personal experience).

Coffee Creamer

Disguising the not very nice/ 'acquired' taste of coffee since 1961.

Cocktails

Same intention as coffee creamer, but this time *fruitifying* our other favorite addictive substance; booze.

Customer Service

Just lovely, aren't they? Even the ones on the other end of the phone with no hope of a tip.

Disney

Minus the Sports Bar, Disney's just about the best place to forget you're even British at all.

Driver's License

When your child reaches the grand, enlightened age of sixteen, you're free to cross off the word 'chauffeur' from your laundry list of parental aliases.

Drive-thru

Drive-thru banks, drive-thru coffee, drive-thru school pickups, drive-thru pharmacies, liquor, voting and even wedding chapels: sore bum, anyone?

Entrepreneurs

Ever thought about starting a window-cleaning business? Milk delivery? How about a pasty stand called 'A Pie Dream?'

Extra-Large Everything

Driveways, cars, beds, ketchup bottles, cups, cinema seats, kitchens...no doubt about it; we certainly get our money's worth.

Expats

These are the kinds of ex's you'll never want to get over.

Fridges

Ice-ice Baby.

Family Values

With lots of emphasis on family values, it won't be long before you find yourself dating your eldest over a milkshake.

Frivolity

America; ah yes, the land where you're encouraged to take your inner child to the playground for some *whee* time.

Gadgets

To live in the land of gadgets; what a turn-on. All hail the UV toothbrush sanitizer, toilet nightlight and smart mug to keep your cuppa warm: tea-tastic.

Good Company

The esteemed list of fellow Brit of Americans include Emily Blunt, Dame Julie Andrews, Sir Anthony Hopkins and, now, Yours Truly.

Gas

The low-priced stuff that fills your car engine, not your pants.

Homegoods

Could you be the most beautiful store in the world?

Half & Half

The clever fusion of milk and cream is ideal for our American-born coffee habit. But is this also Britain's future Milky Way?

Hollywood

Home to America's most famous export, the ever-blooming US movie industry. (We forgive you for duping our US expectations.)

Inexpensive Brands

So you can pretend you're more generous than you actually are.

Incognito

Move to America, start afresh, and give your reputation a well-earned restoration period.

Inspiration

We've plunked ourselves in the land of opportunity, democracy and freedom (or at least so we thought...)

Joints

Cannabis, often smoked in a joint (cannabis cigarette), is fully legal in many US states including the entire West Coast; Washington, Oregon and California. Surely it's high time for those of us in the east too?

Journalists

Undoubtedly feeling more like pantomime narrators since 2016; very entertaining show though.

Jeans

In 1853, a German immigrant living in California named Levi Strauss started selling a type of trouser durable enough for hardworking miners to wear whilst trying to 'hit pay dirt' (digging for gold to you and me). Ever since jeans have arguably become the world's favorite item of clothing. They're a gold mine all of their own, really.

Key-Lime Pie

Humble pie we eat, but bitter? That's a mouth-puckering rebellion from our custard-soaked puddings.

Krispy Kreme Doughnuts

Iced glazed with chocolate, strawberry or cake batter and loaded with sweet, frothy cream. *Mmm*; they kertainly kan make doughnuts.

Kindness

According to the World Giving Index in 2019, the US is ranked as the most generous country in the world. Britain comes in seventh place, which does explain our heightened inferiority complex at each and every holiday occasion.

Leftovers

Go out to eat, doggy-bag the remnants, feed off it for a week, freeze the rest.

Luxury

Ever feel like you've 'made it' because you can wash your hands without getting second degree burns, your kitchen countertop doesn't peel and there's no need to turn the telly down for the sake of the elderly neighbors three doors away?

Libraries

Ah, lovely libraries. Probably the only public warmish indoor space (that bloody drafty air conditioning again) where all present are required to *shush!*

Marshalls

Shopping Mecca since 1956.

Mexican Food

Where you'll quickly discover any J's you see on the menu are merely optical illusions.

Motorhomes

Not quite as glamorous as our tug-along caravans, but still, a pretty efficient way to jolly around gazillions of American miles.

Natural Wonders

Think 'park' with a Brit-brain and you might imagine a green belt to thunk a football around in, damp benches and squeak-to-a-stop-halfway-down-slides. Here, you best pack a tartan rug and flask because a park can involve volcanoes, lakes, woodland, glacier mountains and zoo-worthy wildlife, all squeezed into eight million square miles.

Netflix

Oh goody; there's no need to venture out to entertain ourselves then.

Nightlife

If you haven't yet line danced, pop it on your bucket list.

Ocean

Specifically the Atlantic because it's our Brit of an American yellow brick road.

Over Medium Eggs

Not sure if this specific eggy request would go over too well in a British café...

Orange Trees

The addition of the sun-what with it being a fundamental component in the growth of all living things- means we can attempt to grow all sorts of exotic plants and trees.

Positive People

Presumably the happy result of not getting pissed as much as us.

Parking

So long, park n' ride.

Pharmacies

Sweetie shops for grown-ups.

Quitting Bad Habits

Linger here long enough and you too may be forced to quit all sorts of Britishisms you thought you were permanently saddled with.

Quick Service

Oh yes in theory we love our lazy European-esque lunches, but waiting isn't nearly as fun without the obligatory aperitifs.

Queuing Etiquette

Luckily, our favorite pastime, queuing, is honored here too. Simply take your place in the line and let our forthright American pals sort out any naughty little queue jumpers.

Refills

Automatically giving your child six sugary drinks; *that's* a soda stream.

Red rock

A defining feature of the staggering American landscape. The restaurant's not bad either.

Recliners

They may be over-sized, they may be ugly, but they are addictively cuddly.

Roads

They're big, they're wide and there's no need to reverse park up into a hedgerow in the likely event that you should meet an oncoming car.

Star Quality

Hailing from a tiny island-however mighty-means you're a unique individual with an accent that can win you attention, rates and even cheeky career leg-ups (or overs).

Summer Solutions

You: 'Alexa, what's the American word for boarding school?'
Alexa: 'Summer camps.'

Self-Service Gas Stations

That's one less social interaction to bother with.

TJ Maxx

You suspected that was coming, didn't you?

Thanksgiving

Because there's nothing more we Brits enjoy than a family gathering and a pureed roast dinner, all washed down with lots of tears and plastic cups of cold tea.

Teeth

The iconic white American smile is yours thanks to a much stronger concentration of bleach products available to buy as whitening strips, toothpastes and kits; *brilliant.*

US Citizenship

Dual citizenship; your proudest achievement.

Unions

Giving you the feeling that you can do no wrong at work.

Underage Drinking

The legal drinking age in the US is twenty-one, ours is of course eighteen (thank heavens we grew up in Blighty). But this is excellent news for parents who don't really want to raise drink-dependents. Let's hope our junior Brit of Americans can find a way to buzz-wiser.

Vacation Spots

Aside from the fact that most Americans believe they live in the best country in the world, there's a reason only 42% of US citizens have a valid passport: there's a lifetime worth of exploration right here, especially when you only get five minutes off a year to travel.

Volleyball

Sand instead of pebbles makes the whole sport far less uncomfortable.

Visionaries

Americans tend to focus on the future, which is actually rather sensible, given the fact that it's the more flexible option than our obsession with the past. Before you know it, manifestation will be your new favorite buzzword.

Welcoming

Baked homemade treats, welcome to your new home cards, and all you did was move in. Maybe this is when good neighbors become good friends?

We the People

Even with our British constitutions, let us hope domestic tranquility and perfect union awaits us all.

Wildlife

Because a tame life sounds boring.

Xxx

So long, ambiguous kisses at the end of texts. No, we don't miss fretting over you.

Xmas

Sometimes you've just got to go large, and when, if not at Christmas?

XXL Clothing

Give it five or so years and this accommodating size starts to shrink.

Y'all

The convenient packaging of the words 'you' and 'all.' How did we ever get by without this nifty phrase, y'all?

Yes Ma'am/Sir!

How *polite*!

Yvette

I'm a Y, a homesickness hack, because you've got an expathetic friend in me.

Zest

America; the ultimate way to your zest life.

Zipper

A cuter sounding version of our zip.

Zzz's

Although we Brit of Americans often maintain that our British washable duvet covers are a much more sanitary option than musty-can't-be-bothered-to-dry-clean-comforters, the beds and mattresses themselves really are Big Softies.

Nighty-night.

Dining Out Al Fiasco

'Forget the table manners your parents painstakingly drummed into you as a child; grab a stack of napkins, tuck one in over your shirt and get stuck in. Complete meal by licking sticky fingers and nailing free any stubborn bits of food left in your teeth.
Bon Appetite, old boy.'
-Sue, Colorado/Surrey, feeling liberated, thanks to the chain restaurant experience.

- Discovering a British cafe and reviewing the bangers and mash with the fervor of a *Masterchef* food critic.

- Refusing to chuck peanut shells on the floor at a Texas roadhouse, despite the rest of your dinner companions launching them into the air like confetti.

- Regardless of practice, you're still incapable of holding a cup of soda without recruiting both hands and a good deal of core strength.

- Never being quite sure if you're expected to drink your wine out of a straw too.

- Your non-negotiable dinnertime rule: no phones at the table.

- All you can eat buffets are starting to grow on you.

- You're the only one who translates 'we're going to the best BBQ place in town' as 'expect a Michelin star atmosphere.'

- Never entering an air-conditioned Floridian restaurant in summer without your thickest woolen jumper.

- Your idea of fast food is a waiter hurling a burger towards your parked car a la roller-skates.

- An authentic Indian restaurant makes you feel really at home.

- Server: 'How'd you like your eggs, hunny, fried or scrambled?'
  You: 'Ooh, poached sounds lovely, thanks.'

- Feeling like a particularly sweaty game show contestant as the server fires sixty-six questions at you related to dressings, sides, salads and cooking temperatures.

- Being a bit too liberal with the cinema's popcorn butter dispenser and ending up listening to the movie from the loo.

- The defiant *brit* of you vows to get to the bottom of the stodgy sugar-laden milkshake, even if it leaves you horizontal and fair game for type 2 diabetes.

- Resurrecting your inner-toddler in the crab restaurant as you fasten a paper bib around your neck and prepare to get messy.

- It's always you who gets wedged beside the chatty stranger at the Japanese Steakhouse.

- Repurposing your fork into a tool for scratching initials into to-go boxes (sorry mummy and daddy).

- Asking for 'no ice' and receiving arctic-cold water served in a frozen beaker.

- Your child ignores your hard glare and orders an iced-tea anyway.

- You mostly eat in American diners to channel Olivia Newton-John from *Grease.*

- Ordering four separate glasses of wine because no one else agreed it was best just to get a bottle of wine for the table.

- Thanks to living in Britain, you'll never take a friendly, efficient server for granted again.

- Having a competition to see who can visit the buffet the most.

- You: 'Oh, is that your starter? Sorry, I thought it was the tables' sample platter.'

- Your guilty pleasure involves watching a British visitor tackle a stacked bacon burger with a knife and fork.

- Your pockets are shamelessly stuffed with leftover packets of condiments because they're *freeee!*

- The salad in your dressing likes to play hide-and-seek.

- Only taking teeny bites until the server has been to your table to make sure everything's alright with your meal.

- Feeling like the Lord of the Manor for putting your knife and fork together after finishing dinner.

- Server, setting down the bill: 'Can I get you anything else?' You: 'Time to eat, perhaps?'

- Your idea of live entertainment is the restroom's automatic paper towel dispenser.

- Your American host invites you to help yourself to whatever's in the pantry as you therefore resign yourself to temporary starvation.

- Some nationalities enjoy coffee after dinner, some schnapps, but for you, now, it's got to be antacid medicine.

Love and Marriage: The American Edition

'How the blinking heck am I supposed to date without any pubs?'-
'Big Ben,'
Florida/Manchester, missing our go-to social solution for every occasion.

- Sex appeal is evidentially seaborne; leaving Blighty with the lure of an urchin and landing in the US as some kind of starfish.

- Activity-based dates become an unfortunate reality.

- The only thing reserved about your date is the sign on the dinner table they booked.

- The American you've been dating asks you to 'go steady;' you assume they mean with the *Prosecco* consumption.

- Now you've proudly notched up your first sexual encounter, you finally feel you've grasped what 'foreign exchange' really means.

- Your idea of an aphrodisiac is a passionate argument over whose country is better.

- 'Oh goodness gracious me, he's circumcised, and I *hate* asking for directions.'

- Dinner dates demonstrate they enjoy a hand-to-mouth relationship with food.

- You bring the whine to the relationship; they add the spray-canned cheese.

- You point-blank refuse to copulate outside for fear of being shot.

- You: 'Why do you keep staring at me?'
  Them: 'Because I *love* you!'
  You: 'Right-o.'

- Your American spouse becomes your part-time lover and full-time cultural liaison officer.

- The only joint income in your relationship is your partner's new marijuana habit.

- Hoping your transatlantic romance ends better than Jack and Rose's in *Titanic.*

- Your collection of British-American films has sextupled.

- They quickly discover the way to your heart is learning precisely how you take your tea.

- Prefacing any conversation to do with your childhood with 'a long time ago in a galaxy far, far away...'

- Pillow talk: 'Can you turn the brightness down on your teeth please, dear? I'm trying to sleep.'

- According to your American spouse, telepathy is not a reliable form of communication.

- Thinking 'well, the thought was there,' after they buy you American chocolate.

- Is it normal to unleash every pent-up frustration you've ever had with the USA out on one individual American? (Asking for a friend.)

- You blame being British for all of your character flaws.

- Feeling quietly smug around your British mates now that your other half is an exotic American, especially as they said you'd never mount anything.

- Accepting that both a British and an American dictionary are regrettably necessary if you're ever going to play *Scrabble* together again.

- Having to turn the movie up because you can't hear a word over your partner crying their eyes out.

- Just no: very public and very crowd-pulling marriage proposals.

- You think for safekeeping, your diamond engagement ring ought to be locked away with the rest of the crown jewels.

- Your American's version of fancy pants is wearing their cleanest pair of pajamas to run errands.

- You: 'I have no desire to write my own vows, darling, especially as the Church of England did such a lovely job back in 1662.'

- Promising a free bar to all the female American attendees who come to your wedding wearing a hat.

- You have to file for bankruptcy shortly after Valentine's Day.

- During video calls, your relatives resort to simply nodding, smiling and waving at your spouse.

- Their teen years included summer camps, fishing and ball games, yours-frenzied Mediterranean holidays with mates abroad, underage drinking and plenty of poor choices.

- You're rather pleased that Prince Harry and Meghan Markle give transatlantic marriages such as yours royal connections.

- Your contraceptive modalities involve nagging.

- Whenever they suggest relationship counseling, it never fails to put you in a pissy mood.

- You call your mother-in-law by her first name because you can't pronounce 'mom.'

- If your other half didn't tip so much, you'd be driving a covertible by now.

- Asking the in-laws if their child was born with that baseball cap on.

- Unfortunately, for the special American in your life, if emotional intelligence had been a school subject, you'd have been expelled.

- Hotly debating which country you'll retire to, despite only being in your thirties.

- After years of your selfless tutoring, you're proud to announce your spouse is now conversational in Received Pronunciation and, most impressively of all, Cockney-Rhyming Slang.

A Different Sort of Holiday

'There are over 3.8 million square miles to explore, mum, and I've only got twelve days of annual leave to do it in. So we thought we may as well just stay put for Thanksgiving.'

–Sandra, South Carolina/Yorkshire, sizing up the geographical logistics of her next holibob.

- Thanksgiving; at least there's no need to fret over your gift-giving shortcomings, only culinary.

- After living in the States for decades, you still have no idea what candied yams are.

- On Thanksgiving morning, you often find the kitchen commandeered by a bunch of noisy Americans you hardly know.

- Satisfaction is popping your feet up with a Bucks Fizz and watching the Macy's Day Parade on a random Thursday off.

- Being shamelessly first in line for food, yet still always needing to nuke it.

- Bringing some British culinary civility to the table by axing the mashed potatoes and white buns for proper roasties and Yorkshire pudding.

- Feeling you've got to grips with what going 'cold turkey' means (it's definitely more literal than you thought).

- Mumbling your way through the pre-dinner prayer but making yourself heard for the familiar 'Amen' bit.

- Trying to shield your horrified expression when someone suggests going around the table and sharing what you're grateful for.

- That 'do I/don't I rub her back' dilemma as your American mother-in-law drips happy, grateful tears into her loaded mashed potato.

- Keeping your gratitude list simple but feeling a twinge of guilt for not crying too.

- You have to look in the opposite direction when serviettes are mistaken for tissues.

- Hoping Coronavirus puts an end to hand-holding at prayer time once and for all; too bad, Uncle Randy.

- Spending three days washing up pans you didn't know you had.

- Being a bit pissed and calling your British family at work to wish them a Happy Thanksgiving.

- Trying to devour deviled eggs like canapés and accidentally locking out your jaw.

- Grazing off so many leftovers sandwiches from November to January that you actually start believing your spirit animal is a turkey.

- Doing such a lovely job at Halloween decorating your home with motion-activated witches and dead people that you're too frightened to stay home at night.

- Typically you refuse to wear t-shirts indicating the season but you'll make an exception for '*I'm just here for the boos.*'

- The only apple bobbing games going on are the sliced ones floating around in the dodgy-looking cider.

- You've realized that if you really want to frighten an American, you only need stand in front of them and talk about socialism.

- Sitting outside handing out sweets (as supposed to hiding in your house in the dark) means you're far more American than you ever thought possible.

- Setting off trick-or-treating with your flask of liquor because, of course, Halloween is all about spirits.

- Having a *brit* of a grumble over how expensive and commercialized Halloween is.

- Bulk-buying mahoosive bags of trick-or-treat candy but still managing to run out by 7pm.

- Feeling very naughty indeed for planting an explosive four-foot walking/talking firework at school on November 1st.

- Nicking all the kid's British brands of candy because they couldn't possibly appreciate them as much as you do.

- Spending November with your dentist; it's that root canal time of year.

- You have to give it to the Americans; they do scary much better than us.

- You valiantly offer to put in overtime on July 4th.

- Being the sole British representative on Independence Day, therefore spending the entirety of the barbeque apologizing 88% more than usual.

- Gagging for a cuppa at the 4th July barbeque, but not wanting to be seen drinking the liquid substance that started the whole bloody rebellion off in the first place.

- You use the rather excellent buffalo wings to eat away your feelings of loss.

- Not applying enough sunscreen and ending up a suitably lobster-back shade of red.

- Experiencing the relief of being able to say 'Happy New Year' without detonating a politically-incorrect bomb.

A BRIT OF AN AMERICAN'S GUIDE TO SETTLING OUR CULTURAL DIFFERENCES

Transitioning to America would be much less fraught if those freshly independent Americans back in 1776 hadn't decided to rebel from us so thoroughly well. It's as if some bright scout took a long, thoughtful look at the defeated Brits and said... '*By gum, I've got it! We Americans will become the exact opposite of the Brits, just to make sure we move as far away culturally and economically from the shackles of aristocratic elitism, expensively taxed tea and tediously apologetic personalities as humanly possible.*

'We'll keep the language; we've better things to be getting on with than making up new noises for things. But we shall become the antithesis of every single British characteristic, until all traces of our British origins have been well and truly flushed away. (And to ensure we make it as uncomfortable as possible for the greedy, imperialistic little gits to follow us over here.)'

Here's what those naughty Americans swapped:-

Fear for Fearlessness

Americans: They're now swashbuckling brave. But, really, if you live among earthquakes and polygamy and brown recluse spiders, it's pretty effective I-don't-scare-easily-training.

Brits: We have been known to jump at the sight of our own shadows.

Passivity for Assertiveness

Americans: Sometimes teetering on the brink of aggressiveness to the untrained foreign eye, forthright Americans are an anomaly to our sensitive British natures.

Brits: We instead are usually passive and/or passive-aggressive, having been conditioned from birth to squish any suggestion of sentiment. However, it's difficult to forevermore trap something as intangible as emotion, so it *is* known to explode sideways out of us every now and again in a good 'blow-out,' usually after several drinks and/or external provocation (however unintended).

Conflict Phobia for Conflict Confidence

Americans: Conflict management: A+ (2020 presidential debate aside).

Brits: Conflict management: D. We just need a bit more practice, really, but a stereotypical-forming numbers of us are highly adept conflict-saboteurs, relying instead on honing our manipulation skills to get our way.

Politeness for Authenticity

Americans: Authenticity comes with a warning: Americans are truth-bombers prizing honesty over what they think you want to hear.

Brits: Far too conflict-phobic to even poke the truth, which is why we're universally regarded as polite to a fault.

Subservience for Self Entitlement

Americans: If our Karen so much as breaks a toenail at your house you may need to pay one of those frightening arms-folded- billboard- lawyers to play defensive fisticuffs for you.

Brits: We'd rather eat a crocodile's penis on *I'm a Celebrity... Get Me Out of Here!* than put anyone out on our behalf. Even if it's just asking which aisle the marmalade's in.

Bashful Conversations for Boastful

Americans: Favorite topic: me

Brits: Give us generic topics (like the weather), give us self-deflective conversations (meteorology)? Then you'll begin to see how our cold front melts.

Simple Pleasures for Great Expectations

Americans: Ambitious, goal-oriented, competitive; all of which are sponsored by copious amounts of fancy coffee.

Brits: We aim low, which avoids any disappointment. It's all about wallowing in simple pleasures for us: laundry on the line which the British weather gods allow to dry, a suggestion of sun on our osteoporotic bones or the heavenly combination of dry cake and wet tea.

Common Sense for Rules

Americans: Very safety conscious, lots of (annoying) rules, supposedly as a result of too many self-entitled Karens and the threat of those billboard lawyers.

Brits: Not so much, we lean towards common sense. Or try.

Past for the Future

Americans: Warriors of change.

Brits: Tradition, changeless ceremony and history is our pride, even if foreign onlookers chortle at how we carry on nonsensical 700-year-old roleplays in absurd costumes.

Old for the New

Americans: Young and lusty, just getting started.

Brits: Crusty and tired; we've earned a rest after being rather impressive for a thousand years of imperialistic efforts, industrial revolutionizing and fighting with all our foreign friends.

Self-Deprecation for Self-Love

Americans: Self-love and self-care and self-confidence and self-everything is the ultimate aim of any self-respecting American.

Brits: We too love a bit of self (flagellation).

Awkwardness for Self-Assurance

Americans: Embarrassment: a state that's way out west for most Americans.

Brits: Cringing, awkwardness and humiliation are primeval British states, easily activated, even by the most risk-averse, comfort-zoned among us. That's most Brits until death, unfortunately.

Deary me. It's no wonder we can feel like square pegs in round holes. Our American friends appear to have been first in line for some of the more desirable human qualities. But here we are, exposed to examples of how to embody self-empowerment, passion and exceptional productivity. It's never too late, you know.

Let's be honest. Even the American characteristics we love to hate we're still slightly jealous of. Doesn't skirting with obnoxiousness seem far less exhausting than a lifetime doomed to people-pleasing? It's a bit like a human effectiveness bootcamp that you can't leave. After the initial desperate pleas to send you home, they eventually break you in.

The good news is, a bit of foreign-fusion can have wonderful implications for your life. Hark at my friend Sue from Cornwall. After terming herself as a 'plodder-alonger' all the while she lived in Britain, she's quite the opposite now. Submerged in this you-can-do-it culture her dormant entrepreneurial spirit has been ignited. She's pulling in sums she feels she'd never have accomplished back home.

Then there's Nigel from Oxford/Texas. He was clinically depressed before expatting, crumbling into alcoholism. Yet now you'll find him every Sunday morning, glistening with a mixture of tears and joy, having apparently found God lurking in one of those mega-churches.

Finally, there's Amy from East Sussex/Boston. She runs workshops to help others communicate with pets and plants telepathically. You can see how her British roots (*hopefully- if- I- just- think- it- I- won't- have- to- say- it*) may have had a hand in growing this particular skill to extend to all life forms.

These peeps may *appear* British, but the metamorphosis is happening inside nonetheless. If you haven't yet seen any signs of your own evolvement, rest assured its coming. America's probably not done with the breaking-you-down process quite yet. Yep, it has to be said; we really are the lucky ones.

Born N' Raised Brit of Americans

'It's a strange thing for a Brit to grow an American from babyhood. Your children may look like you but they don't sound like you, they don't act like you and their childhood is completely different to how yours was. As often as you can, take them back to Britain to a) show that US dentists really are our friends; b) how to negotiate stiles wearing corduroy and c) to offer irrefutable proof that some of us really do live in houses pre-dating Pocahontas.'

-Fred, California/Kent, who often scans his own grown-up children for any rogue signs of their British heritage.

- With hindsight, you're not at all sure that naming your America-born baby something frightfully British was altogether the best start as a loving parent.

- Bolting from hospital with your newborn son before the pediatrician can mention the dreaded c-word.

- 'Dummy' becomes a banned word in your house, so your baby has to suck on a pacifier instead.

- Purchasing sixteen types of biscuits so you can teach your kids all about the technicalities of tea dunking.

- Your child gets an ADHD diagnosis aged three; admittedly it *is* pretty handy having a readymade excuse for all his naughtiness.

- Applying for your child's British passport just in case they ever fall on hard times.

- The day you make a peanut butter and jelly sandwich for your kid is the day you become 20% more American and 20% less British.

- Your eleven-year-old is on their second cavity, third bed and fourth iPad.

- Getting suspicious looks from the pediatrics receptionist because you always manage to get little Penelope's birthday backward.

- Supporting your baby's fine motor skills with a tea set.

- You, on family movie night: 'Right, what's it to be- *Paddington, Peter Rabbit* or *Christopher Robin*?'

- Feeling powerless to prevent your children from becoming both very much seen and very much heard.

- Telling your mini-Americans not to breathe a word as you approach the UK customs officer at Heathrow.

- Periodically marveling at how you ever produced such self-assured offspring with all the social subtleties of…Americans, oddly enough.

- The age-old debate of whether to eat bacon with hands or cutlery is alive and well in your household.

- Your three-year-old British nephew appreciates fine-dining far more than your tween- aged American daughter.

- Forks become shovels.

- Buying your kids expensive organic multivitamins to forgive them for their culinary trespasses, for they know not what they eat.

- Both your children hate *Marmite.*

- Your kids use egg soldiers to reenact the War of Independence.

- 'Use your serviette, darling.'
  'My whaaat?'

- You: 'No, darling, 'mum' doesn't have an 'o' in it.'

- Junior doesn't do any of the chores you wrote down; apparently, joined-up handwriting is about as helpful as leaving instructions in Arabic.

- If you weren't so cripplingly British, you'd actually campaign for school uniforms.

- NB-Yellow school buses, field trips and British temperaments are not a good mix.

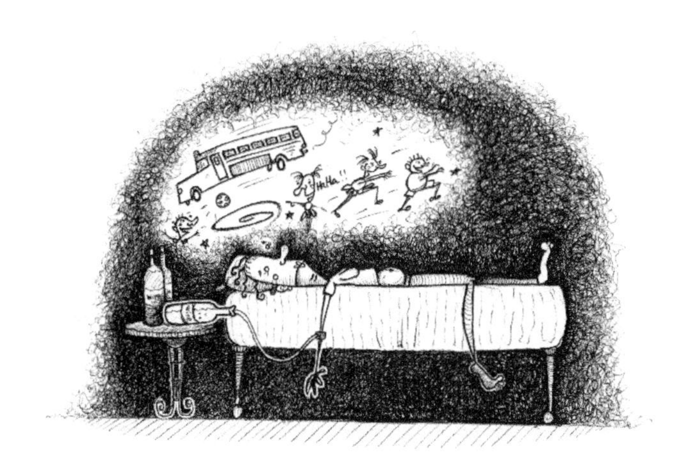

- Having to donate 90% of your precious weekends to your kid's sporting competitions.

- The kids ask if they have to be over twenty-one to eat *Wine Gums.*

- Your child earns an unfortunate reputation as a hypochondriac after grazing their knee at school and asking for a plaster.

- Refusing to hire an English tutor for little Henry because you just feel he should just accept his weaknesses.

- Crying into your child's common core third-grade math homework because you can't understand it either.

- You think Mother's Day in your household ought to be celebrated in March *and* May, but your kids are having none of it.

- You still can't help calling the Principal *Headmistress.*

- Compared to American school dinners, the gloppy semolina you had at school doesn't seem half as threatening now.

- Having your children's friends over for tea and turning into a Finishing School Mistress.

- Adding extra 'u's to words and therefore helping your child flunk a second-grade spelling test.

- Receiving a dirty look from your child across the dinner table and remembering they had World History today.

- Hoping Junior Reserve Officer Training Core makes up for years of your unsuccessful attempts to pull mini-Brit-of-an-American into line.

- You're still not totally sure if a braid is the same thing as a plait.

- In a bid to avoid your sorry state, every time your children unnecessarily apologize they too have to put a dollar in the jar.

- Your child frequently laughs at you for your die-hard British pronunciations.

- Earning a voodoo reputation among your children's friends for cooking toads, faggots and spotty dicks.

- You: 'So if I throw you one of those Sweet Sixteen parties, will you promise to be just that?'

- Quickly learning that British terms of affection such as 'little shits' and 'knobheads' are not quite as well-loved over here.

- Divulging your wild student antics in the hope your teen chooses a British university over a US college thirty times as expensive.

- Your children won't let you kiss them anymore because they say you smell of tea.

- After planning a London pub crawl to celebrate your child's eighteenth birthday, your cool points are temporarily reinstated.

- You buy your kids an ancestry DNA kit for Christmas to remind them of their loyalties.

- Your favorite way to wind your daughter up is to talk about pencils and rubbers around her boyfriend.

WILDLIFE AND WEATHER WOES

'Unless he's Winnie the Pooh, I'd rather not come nose to nose with a bear.'

– Rachel, Florida/Gloucestershire, currently hibernating from her furry neighbors.

- Seeing a suspicious-looking spider spindled in a tree and promptly terminating your hike, despite only having just got out of the car.

- After being stung by a jellyfish, eaten alive by fire ants and violated by ticks you feel you thoroughly deserve your American citizenship now.

- Having pretty much no idea what any plants, birds or trees are called in these warmer climes.

- Swimming in the ocean and feeling like you're in a particularly biting episode of *Shark Tank.*

- Alright mosquitoes, you win; no more camping for me.

- After making a bit of a show of yourself trying to evacuate an entire beach, you can now happily spot the difference between shark and dolphin fins.

- You're pretty sure that toxic bug household spray is just as effective at killing the British species as it is all the other unwanted creepy crawlies.

- Once upon a time, you checked the bed sheets for spiders before you got in, now you check the loo for snakes before you sit down.

- The once-feared shed in your parent's garden in Blighty now seems tame: put 'em up, daddy-long-legs!

- Unknowingly swimming in a lake swarming with alligators and dining off the increasingly exaggerated story for the rest of your life.

- Being too frightened to keep the sliding doors open in case a snake, bear or coyote pops in for tea.

- Thanks to the encroaching local wildlife, your beautifully designed Zen garden is anything *but* relaxing.

- American Mystery Number 4,867,099: Why do Americans shrill at the sight of cockroaches when they're the least of your wildlife worries?

- Pah! To think, you used to be afraid of walking through a field of cows.

- Now you know what sunshine feels like, you realize most Brits back home really are SAD; the poor cold buggers are suffering from year-round Seasonal Affective Disorder.

- You prepare for the oncoming tornado by popping on your anorak.

- Discovering flamingoes are not the only ones to go that particular shade of pink under the sun.

- You know all about nor'easters.

- You're American enough now to change the door wreath with each new season.

- Humidity is not your friend.

- Your family stages an intervention over your unhealthy relationship with seasonal candles.

- Whatever happened to the good old days when just a flurry of slushy snow caused the entire country to grind to a halt?

- 'I'm so homesick for Britain that I even miss the weather'- said no Brit ever.

- You still pop up your brolly during a lightning storm.

- You believe your body hair means you have an inbuilt sun defense mechanism equating to SPF Factor 8000.

- Warm Floridian Christmases just won't do.

- Experience has taught you the difference between heat exhaustion and heatstroke.

- The best thing about a hurricane threat is the hunkering down bit.

- Your impressive party trick is being able to drink hot black tea outside in savagely high temperatures.

- Realizing there's no need to rush to the shops to fight over tins of soup before a hurricane; everyone will leave the nutritious non-perishables on the otherwise empty shelves for you.

- Regaling your British family with tales of your heroism during the tornado, even though you were cowered in your closet spitting out obscenities throughout the whole thing.

- Thinking the Americans missed Jesus' memo about the danger of building houses on sand.

- You're in a constant state of moaning that it's either too hot or too cold.

- Knowing you're becoming more American than recommended when you're disappointed a hurricane gets downgraded to a tropical storm and doesn't hit your county after all.

- The only time you really appreciate the air conditioning in your American home is when you're back in Britain during a heatwave.

- Thinking the weather is just like the Americans themselves; never a dull moment.

SOUNDING A BRIT TOO AMERICAN?

Have you ever forgotten the British translation for something because you're so used to saying it the American way? Are British words like queue, cupboard and loo becoming as neglected as a 'butter' knife at an American dinner table? These are warning signs that you, me old chum, are becoming less and less British and more and more American.

Your British accent may still be in pristine order (after all, accents are pretty stubborn blighters to shift post-childhood). Yet American-English is starting to crawl all over your vocabulary, phraseology and even swarming into your pronunciation.

It is an almost imperceptible process as we're left to our own devices, alone and adrift in a sea of Americans. It's a little bit like a lobster plunked into a pan of cold water on the stove and slowly adjusting to the incremental rise in temperature, clueless that it's being boiled alive until death.

But fear not because the very test to assess your American/ English linguistic-mess is here. Just pop a tick beside all the statements that apply to you and we'll see just how befuddled/ Americanized you've gotten (excuse me; *got*).

1. You pronounce 'schedule' 'sked-dule' instead of 'scched-dual'

2. You sometimes say 'I know it' when agreeing with someone's point of view because the British translation 'I know' doesn't seem nearly as robust

3. You've stopped calling cashiers 'love'

4. 'Period' makes you think of full stops

5. You say 'I need a...' when, really, you just 'want a ...'

6. You've happily managed to switch out saying 'sorry' for 'excuse me'

7. You often start conversations that don't revolve around the finer details of the current cloud arrangements in the sky

8. You've gathered Americans don't feel the need for anyone's blessing, so you only say 'bless you' if someone sneezes

9. You frequently end conversations by wishing people nice things, such as that old-cringe-inducing-chestnut 'have a great day!'

10. 'I'm done' has replaced 'I'm finished'

11. Your 'T's sound migh'd' similar to 'D's

12. 'A-loom-e-num,' or 'Al-u-minion?' (If you pronounce it the first way, give yourself a tick)

13. Fanny-packs don't tickle your funny bones quite as much anymore

14. Ending a conversation with 'off you go' sounds a *brit* harsh

15. British words like 'post,' 'tidy' and 'rubbish' sound quaint and cutesy

16. Your pub banter is not what it once was

17. When you need to pause a conversation to verify what was just said, you're more likely to say 'wait' than 'hold on'

18. The sizeable distance between what you say and what you mean is beginning to shrink

19. You're more likely to say 'where are you at?' than 'where are you?'

20. Sweet little British children, oh how their accents enchant you

21. When someone thanks you, an automatic 'you're welcome' tumbles out of your mouth, because you can't just leave their gratitude stagnating in the air between you

22. Your British family visit and look to you to translate. Luckily for them, you speak fluent redneck and can tell them 'I'm happier than a tornado in a trailer park' does indeed mean he's very pleased

23. You often drop the 'the' before saying things like 'I'm going to watch (the) football' or 'I'm going to (the) hospital'

How'd you do?

18 or More Ticks: Bri-Merican

Now I don't want you to panic, but you're a little more than a Brit of an American. You're a Lot of an American (very specific diagnosis, I know). This may or may not be welcome news. But let's just crack on with why it's marvelous: the American language is punchy, powerful and has less formality and silly nonsensical stuff to it (as endearing as our British-English may be). Using this new fandangled American language can in turn manipulate how you feel, how you're received, even your personality and very identity. Direct language, direct you, hey? You're like this open-minded, confident Bri-Merican Being, with a whole new world perspective, experiencing two realities, having transcended the geographical, cultural and linguistic confines of dear old Blighty.

Maybe you're like me, with a crisp British accent but a dictionary swarming with Americanisms, or, in the process of noticing your accent free-styling into some strange coagulation of British/American. Or perhaps you're one of those especially cool Bri-Mericans who can switch their accent from full-on British to full-on American, dependent on who you're talking to.

Whichever category you fall into, you have linguistically assimilated. How very clever of you.

10-17 Ticks: Two for the Price of One

You, me ol' lobster-back pal, are starting to turn pink with heat. You're probably at the stage where you're questioning Who Am I? (A worthy question for anyone to ask, quite frankly.) You barely notice that you're picking up an American phrase here and there, to be understood, mind, just to inspire a sense of camaraderie amongst the locals, you reason. You may be conversational in your local American dialect, but you're still distinctively British.

Although you may feel as if you're suffering from an identity crisis, know that you're just going through the messy, confusing bit and once through this, you'll blossom into a full-blown Bri-Merican. In the meantime, enjoy the best of both worlds.

9 Ticks and Under: Still British (Possibly Terminally)

Could you be a recent British export? Were you well-passed middle-age when you expatted here? Or perhaps you're living with other Brits and therefore remain linguistically unscathed. Maybe you're just so immovably British that we should refer to you as 'The Resistance.' The good news is our American friends have huge affection for quirky Brits. You're a rare breed over here and therefore even more of an authentic treasure. If you're single and ready to mingle you shouldn't have any trouble snagging at least a date (although, if I were you, I'd read the Love and Marriage chapter pretty carefully).

I'm sure any distant ancestors who arrived on these foreign shores courtesy of the Mayflower circa1620 are immeasurably proud of you. Here you are, sitting pretty, in all your unsullied Britishisms, not just a mere settler but a *Cultural Enhancer.*

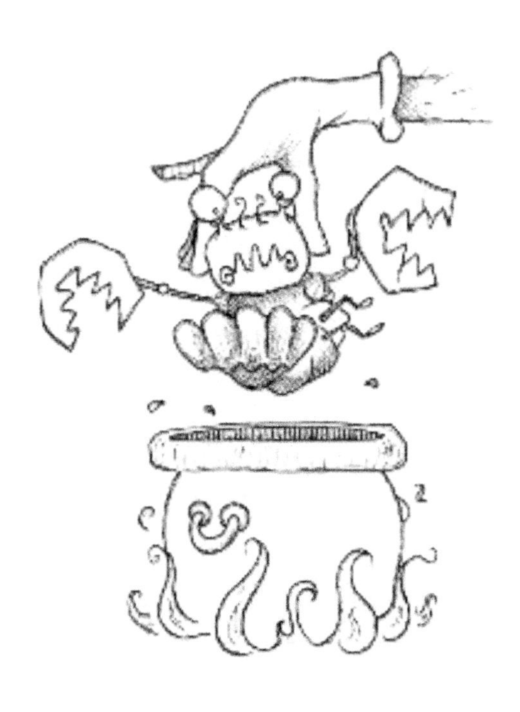

VACAY VACAY: BACK HOME TO BRITAIN

'Occasionally I go home and remember why I left. But more often than not I experience utopian Britain; craggy castles, sun-soaked beer gardens, salty vinegar on thick, newspaper-wrapped chips, and my heart burns when it's time to leave. But could I go back permanently? More to the point, would they have me back?'
- Katie, Pennsylvania/Cheshire, wrestling with that 'could I go back?' question all we Brit of Americans ponder.

- Yes! Discovering your assigned plane seat is next to a quiet sleepy Brit.

- Pushing the recline button on your plane seat *before* the meal and feeling gloriously American.

- Skipping towards the UK passport control at the airport, buoyed by all the lovely tourist pictures of London on the way.

- Driving past picturesque green countryside and trying to suppress the urge to burst into a William Wordsworth soliloquy.

- Now you know from hard-won travel experience that pub stands for Perfect Utopian Britain.

- Seeing thatched roofs, village churches and red letterboxes with excited American eyes and begging your pelvic floor muscles not to let you down.

- The first place of interest you visit takes six hours to meander through and is called *Sainsbury's.*

- Phew! *Finally* you've got the hang of driving on the right.

- Your idea of getting dirty involves narrow British country lanes and big tractors smacking you with mud.

- You *always* try to get into the car on the wrong side.

- Winding up two counties north of your intended destination because you couldn't get enough of your British-accented Sat-Nav.

- Completely getting the gin craze now that you've sampled mother's ruin in a range of flavors that mask the nauseating taste.

- Now Wellington-booted and rooted on British soil, your children's American accents become alarmingly obvious.

- Buying nineteen items at the shop and smashing four on the pavement outside because you forgot it was Bring Your Own Bag every day.

- Discovering how wholly under-qualified you are as a grocery bag packer.

- No one's excited about your accent.

- Watching an action movie with your emotively deadpan relatives and still managing to cry.

- Picking out soggy bits of old dinner from the kitchen sink while feeling really homesick for America.

- The more American your kids become, the more British castles, attractions and palaces you drag them around.

- It may be July, but you're going to light the log fire nevertheless. *Brrr.*

- Challenging an old dear to a knife duel in the teashop for the honor of the last pot of clotted cream.

- Older relatives interact with your children like curious museum artifacts.

- Being physically unable to leave the country until you've eaten fish and chips, Indian takeout, pub roast, kebab, Chinese carryout (*with* prawn crackers) and all the other healthy dishes you've yearned for.

- Flashing the waiter a very apologetic smile as your American dining companions fail to grasp the concept of a *set* menu.

- A single bag of crisps doesn't even touch the sides of your hunger anymore.

- Your favorite G-word to capitalize on is *Greggs.*

- Feeling like your time in the US has all been for nothing when your mate down the pub says you sound just as British as the day you left.

- Giving yourself full permission to digress behaviorally to the age you were when you left the UK.

- You buy enough underwear in *Marks & Spencer* to see you through until 2063.

- Getting handed back 50 pence coins and pounds no longer in tender and therefore feeling like an outcast in your own homeland.

- Finding it impossible to have more than a two-minute conversation with a stranger without mentioning the fact that you live in America.

- Yes, you talk to strangers now.

- Doing your *brit* for British tourism by filling up American friend's social media feeds with pictures of half-timbered British villages.

- You're OK with Brexit-even Megxit-but *Pub*exit? Closing down your local really does take the biscuit. Or pint.

- Now you see it so clearly: Britain was not designed for cars.

- Signing up for an annual overseas *National Trust* membership, even though you won't be back again for at least six years.

- Explaining to any American travel companions the London tube rules: 'stare into space and don't say a word.'

- Going to the cinema mainly so you can guzzle pick 'n' mix in the dark.

- Your I-could-stay-here-forever moment consists of the Sunday papers, a glass of red and the aromatic promise of roast lamb.

- Saying to your Americanized kids, 'now this is what *real* chocolate tastes like.'

- Admiring how smart and fashionable the Brits are (but perhaps the Americans have got a point about our teeth).

- Relishing whole complete doors to cover your genitalia in public loos which mean no need to wrangle your jeans back on from a squatted position.

- You shop in *Joules, John Lewis* and *Poundland* to feel extra British.

- Getting in a spirited debate with a local down the pub, who dares to ridicule the Americans (secretly you agree with everything he says, but only you and your green card have earned the right to criticize).

- Monster-munching your way through as many crisp packets as you can because you can't possibly squeeze any more into your luggage.

- You're the only one onboard crying taking off from a very wet, very grey British airport.

You've Changed!

'Has America irrevocably changed me? Have I got lost in Her vast landscape? Has America's confrontational nature chipped away at me for so long that somewhere along the way, the American in me became my new normal? I think it's more than likely.'

- Jeremy, New York/London, less convinced nowadays of his retirement plan to spend half his year back in the UK.

- You've gotten much better at eye gazing.

- Your British loved ones say 'hello stranger' when you phone home.

- Half the t-shirts you own say things about you.

- You've stopped putting unstamped Christmas cards in neighbors' mailboxes.

- You're a lot more decisive and therefore make ridiculous decisions you have to live with much quicker.

- Cutting your alcohol units in half…

  …but doubling up on your caffeine.

- Finally getting the point; everyone can wear tennis shoes.

- There are several lightly used assertiveness self-help books on your shelf.

- Just like the swollen bunion on her left foot, your American mother-in-law accepts you now as a permanent fixture.

- You're more than happy to talk about money…

  …and religion.

- 'Dressing gown' begins to sound frightfully posh, like something you'd wear to a Ball, not bed.

- Your mealtimes have migrated to an earlier time zone too.

- You've learned to cook because necessity is the mother of invention.

- You start calling God 'the Universe' because it sounds more inclusive and spiritually-correct.

- You believe it's about time you started letting people know when they have food stuck in their teeth.

- Having to think when someone asks who the current British Prime Minister is.

- The pizza in your freezer gets permanent residency.

- You know now that the Superbowl has nothing to do with super bowlers.

- Nowadays you own more strategically-placed sunhats than umbrellas.

- You trade your mini in for a minivan.

- You're a Republican sympathizer these days; anything with the consecutive words 're' and 'pub' gets your vote.

- Your favorite mug combines the British and American flags because if you didn't blend you'd break.

- Nowadays you wear flats, not live in them.

- Of course there's no room for your car in your triple garage, don't be absurd.

- Your certificates are framed for positive reinforcement.

- Your new cure-all is a mani and pedicure.

- Yoga, meditation and/or vigorous exercise are your mature responses to Americanisms you still haven't come to terms with.

- You evolve by attending wellness workshops and hugging strangers who cry.

- Your journal lets you open up.

- You can't be bothered to correct your child's American pronunciations anymore.

- You're not convinced you could live full time in Britain again and actually walk to the shops.

- It's pretty gross remembering how you used to put butter in your sandwiches instead of mayonnaise.

- Your British mates use you as an Agony Aunt.

- You notice your opinions become your own, not the general consensus of everyone else belonging to your socio-economic category.

- It's not just the footie team you support, even you have the occasional goal now.

- You're not sure your neglected yard deserves to be called a garden.

- Retirement becomes your illusive version of the American Dream.

- You spend a lot more time brushing than blushing.

- Thinking how endearing it is, calling a drink 'fizzy.'

- You're able to effectively complain now (well, via email anyway).

- These days you're more likely to load a magazine than read one.

- 'Better out than in' is your new mantra.

- Ditching a string of kisses at the end of text messages for a string of Emojis instead.

- You have double the amount of American friends (four) as you do British (two).

- You're known as mommy or daddy to your pet.

- After ten-plus years of living stateside, you give back by starting a British expat group.

- You're beginning to entertain existential thoughts such as, 'it was my destiny to move to America.'

- You may be on the turn, but you'll always set the world to rights by popping on the kettle.

Conclusion

If this conclusion were a scene, it'd be a British pub at the end of the night. Yep, that's right, happy bumbling *carnage.* Mr. Brit would be slinging his arm around Mr. America's neck and saying, 'Mate, I bloody-well *love you!*'

It's true. As much as our innate imperialistic DNA sets us up to spar with the odd few hundred grating aspects of American culture, we're here. And all the while America works her magic on us, even as we wrangle bouts of homesickness.

One thing I've learned from my American Adventure is that being stateside forces you to take a good hard stare at the luggage you brought over. And I don't mean the sixty-four jars of *Marmite*, the hundred smushed choccie bars nor the *Hula Hoops* we smuggled back after visiting Britain. I mean the intangible things Britain lets us hold on to that America doesn't-gum disease, aging gracefully, underdeveloped communication skills, self-sabotaging habits-that sort of thing. Thanks for prizing those off us, America. *Much better.*

Your own unique swirly brand of British/Americanness is a gift to this country. The very glorious essence of America is that most of us are from somewhere else anyway. We get to consciously create anew, together, in this big melting pot of celebrated differences.

Me? Oh I'm with tipsy Mr. Brit up there...I bloody love America. I bloody love Ameri*cans*. Although I'm challenged most days and can work myself up into the perfect storm over all the usual grievances, the USA has squeezed the very best out of me. I believe in the spirit of this country and hope to make America a proud parent, to grow old here (providing my health insurance is up to the job) because I know Lady Liberty certainly ain't done with me yet.

Pop on over to visit me at Yvette Durham Author on Facebook. I'd love to hear your thoughts on living stateside. Thanks so much for reading, and long may you reign as unofficial British Ambassador in your wee patch of America.

Printed in Great Britain
by Amazon

37106779R00088